Feel It Still

By John Tanner

Feel It Still

First Published 2020
Copyright © 2020 John Tanner

Cover Photo @ 2020 Abby Ready

All rights reserved

I dedicate this book to Séan Phillip Tanner and Daniel James Tanner.

They are my sons and my heirs to this wonderful throne. They inherit the world and all of its wonders.

They own all of the key ingredients for great lives. I thank them for what they give by just being here.

Contents

Contents (Cont.)

Contents (Cont.)

1 2 3 4 5

One, Two, Three, Four, Five

I was a man alive

Six, Seven, Eight, Nine, Ten

Never see that man again

I was really living then

Big job, speedy car

Had dives, then 'the bends'

I reached up so high

Then tumbled, from height

Gave it all, to lose

Found a world, denied

Gave it all, to view

One, Two, Three, Four, Five

Sin bin's here for life

At least I have tried

Past trouble and signs

My biggest dream, flew

As high as I could

Now have dreams a-new

As far as I should

53rd State

Have we finally succumbed
To those distant cousins?

Obese in every big street
Big cholesterol burger buns

Hidden sugar, makes fat fun
Bigger is better, American way

Heart Attack & wine may be OK
Because tanned fat can sway

White fat, just go away
Go away, on holiday

Memphis loves your thunder haze
Squeeze in, at the USA!

Another

It's another week starting

Over again and over too soon

Then we're in again as it's parting

What have you got to lose?

Not much & then nothing

Too quick again, too short a fuse

Time's temper can't stop mocking

Are you a bit bemused?

The old clock is only rocking.

No help if you're confused

As Time Goes By

Listen to their sighs

Huff and puff all day

Watch their downward eyes

Too rarely, hooray

People-watch today

Are they glad to be?

Do their lives feel grey?

Inwardly, make hay?

If inside, they clap?

Are their thoughts shiny?

At home, do they laugh

Laughter's for sharing

Billions

Our world now houses

Seven point eight billion.

Billions of lost souls

How are we so lonely?

Seven point eight billion

We just need to talk?

Stop making babies

Just go for a walk.

Blue Sky

Look up, at blue sky

Its beautiful grace

Perhaps you wonder why

Internal embrace

The future is bright

We are so lucky

As children, running

Clicking heels, laughing

Know not how or why

Too busy, living

Too busy, having

Too busy, giving?

Bored

It's hard, being bored

In a broken body

It's hard, being thrown

Into a broken body

Waking, paralysed

Can't move a muscle

Harder if you're born

To a broken body

Only miss what's gone?

Caged Birds

Caged birds can sing

Better than the free

Than those on the wing

Caged sing for their tea

Sing for their captors

Yearning to be free

Yearn to fly free skies

All that they can be

Carried Away

We're carried, away

There's no going back

We must go forward

Done *that* piece of track

We're carried, away

Life always does that

We might go astray

Just keep working at...

At Terminal One

The one in the sky

No creamy jam scones

No more asking why

Last carried, away

Clay Pigeons

All of the clay pigeons

Thrown up, then fly out

For privileged practice

Hear ambition shout

History's clay pigeons

All men, marched over

Promotions, notions

Time's unknown shoulders

Smell, criminal chance?

Smell the privilege

Filthy rich romance

Fuelled by clay pigeons

Clipped

We all possess wings

Some of us will fly

All of us can sing

As we wonder why

Some of us can cry

We all have tear ducts

Do you let it fly?

Or hold nose, and flush

Your young wings, not clipped?

Quick – run for the bus

Life's too quick to miss

Ride the sky for us

Clouds

Up there, so peacefully

What's above, below?

No rush, earthly hurry

"Cloud, just looking down

We're below, what's up there?

Do you rain your tears?

And thunder, your frowns?"

"Cried over earth for years!

Watched you, like breakdowns

Man's follies, been & gone

Shame, what we've witnessed

Fear what's yet to come

Man's follies, no finesse"

Concentrated Goodness

This is what, we need.

We are "the bee's knees."

Some believe that this

Is reference to the fact

That bees carry pollen

In sacks on their knees.

The expression therefore

Means concentrated goodness.

Courage

Here I lie again

So much more to give

Bed with bladder pain

I just have to live

Get up, to give them

What they've given me

Love's encouragement

A reason to be

Here I sit again

So much more to give

Chair with bladder pain

I just have to live

Covered With Heaven

Covered with heaven

With each touch or smile

I once enjoyed both

Took them, gratis

More free gifts of youth

The free gifts of love

I didn't even know

One day they'd just go

Nobody told me

We all, have limits

We just do not see

Aiming to be 'in it'

Covered with heaven

Don't see, 'till sight fades

Life is unleavened

We just learn too late

Creepy Crawly

Out in the garden, by the hedge, live some creepy crawlies.

Mr Skinny Legs, is right there.

Dark, skinny, long, legs, make his illusion of massive.

All predators are scared of Old, Mr Skinny Legs.

House flies should be - he catches, then eats them up – yum!

He goes to great lengths, to catch flies.

Mr Skinny Legs is quite, the strategic genius, in his quest for a filling meal of flies.

He spends, most of his time around his house, spinning webs.

Where and when he sleeps, is one of the world's great mysteries!

Mr Skinny's webs are made of the most beautiful and fine silk, made exclusively by himself.

His silk is made in his silk glands, with the help of the spinnerets.

Spinnerets are special organs, that allow him, to decide what type of thread he needs for this web.

Mr Skinny Legs is a true artisan, the likes of which, people no longer seem to need.

It takes up to an hour for Mr Skinny Legs to weave a complete web.

Miss Roly Spikes also lives in the garden.

If approached by a predator, she does what her name suggests, rolls into a prickly ball,

Mr Tunnel tunnels underground, to avoid approaching, hungry birds.

While Mr Tunnel escapes the birds, Granny Fly-Up, dodges the local toms, as described by her name, as do her many progeny.

How they make her proud, with their witty speed of flying bobs and weaves.

Meanwhile, Mr Tunnel is busy airating the garden and more besides

COVID 19

A new virus

Hit town last month

Or something.

It is fatal

To the dying

And bad for the ill.

Please do not panic

New normal prospect

More frightening than visors.

Cripple Street

I'm not up Shit Creek

Just down Cripple Street

It's fine week to week

It's fine as seconds fly

The same as before

Thin slice of life, bye

Zooms past, wanting more,

Wise now, we haven't died

Look what's going down

Hear that money scream

Buying care or crowns

It is how it seems

Expensive wheelchairs

Don't want, but need

Can't run, so won't hide

That's how need feels

Right down Cripple Street

Cupid

Cupid only fired once

He hit us both, so well

We must've been in bed

Ours, not to lie and dwell

He turned, both our heads

In that Tooting flat

We were fit and happy

Enter stage Cupid

Like thunder, clapping

'Fall in love,' said Cupid

We did! Now we're four!

That's what we came for

Cupid's job is done

We're here, now we're more

Dad and Me

They thought you were drunk

They think I am daft

Like I speak in tongues

For you, it's all past

You died of Cancer

Doctors failed to see

Doctors were just chancers?

Counting their money

Each organ, riddled

Bowel, lungs, heart, brain

You were world diddled

Now we cry in vain

Thought you, had MS

But they failed to check

Said you had MS

We know, you were best.

Daniel

We love you, Daniel

Forever Daniel

So much, it's hard to say

We love you, Daniel

Our Son, Daniel

Tomorrow, and today

Everyone loves Daniel

He'll grow to change the world

He'll be the man who'll

Fix all, in his new world

No one knows the plan

None but Daniel

In five months, he will be one.

Days Away

Friends don't come with age

Illness turned them away

I turn o'er a blank page

Can't waste another day

Breathing, I must make hay

Benefits now, no wage

That day's gone, so today

Many colours, no more beige

Seeing upsides, each morn

Each day, the joy goes on

No roses, and no thorns

Always thinking, I've won

Dung

Are we as Dung Beetles?

On a sphere of dung?

Try not to be eaten

Try not to be stung

Is this universal

This dung beetle life?

This is no rehearsal

Life smells very nice

When you're used to it

Royals' ermine furs

You don't smell the dung

Fauntleroy's bounce curls

Clouds are elephants?

Nine planets, the herds?

Dung earth's, heaven bent

Run by accountants

Bright Spark

For Séan P Tanner

You were born, ear first

Hearing things, for months

To this fun, with thirst

You could wait, no more

Onto this stage, burst

You'll shoot, and will score

You're finally here

Winning the races

And learning, in cheer

You're going places

Zooming through chases

Cracking the cases

Light up their faces

Earth Needs Peace

All we need is peace.

War's horror, always been

Enough bombs to destroy all.

All we need is peace.

All we need is peace.

War bends generations

Fathers & sons die for belief.

All we need is peace.

All we need is peace.

The odds were on

In infinity you were to be.

All we need is peace.

They've killed the best

Destroying the earth

Now time for the rest

To rise up, peace's birth

Fake News and Mind Games

Why did he deny?

The toxic seed was sown

So climat, has climbed

Ruthless industry foams.

Why on Earth, Brexit?

Just weak politics

Britain's no nexus

Now it's Brorific.

Earth's 'free' world, just groans

'Neath power's corruption

Our votes beget moans

Regret, no justice.

No higher correction

Democracy rules?

Where's our connection

Knaves still canvass fools.

Feel Warm?

How do you feel now?

Now that oceans rise

Will you pause to bow?

With icebergs melting

The years seem shorter

The seas seem mortal

Our snowfall just coughs

Running to stand still

Just there killing seals

They have been ripped off

We've sown, but children...

Nothing left to reap?

The seas are deeper

Now we have to deal

Time goes with the flow

So we must act now

Before islands sink

Pull now, from the brink.

For God's Sake

We built God's houses

All around this place

Where we'll be nearest

To sing, in God's face

We love God far more,

More than them, and you

Look at our Lux' cars

Look at our Guilt Pew

Come to church to see

Big bums, faith anew

Praise them, for God's Sake

The great, holy queue.

Found

If you have found love, real love

For your very first time, the one

Don't look down, they're above

They will be never gone

Busy fitting like a glove

Will be there from dusk to dawn

And from morn to yawn

Love found you both – you won!

Heat

Used to love summer

The heat, the suntans

The summer dresses fair

Summer dresses

Flew past, as sun shone

I miss the guesses

Now in heat, weakness

In sunshine, blindness

Spirit stays, strengthened

Summer clouds, slow pass

Summer dresses, float

MS humid, hot bath

Now summer's wasted

Weather's cruel bias

Temp-like, I'm basted

Hope

Hope is free of charge

With no guarantees

With hopes, small or large

Freedom or world peace

We hope all the time

We hope for money

Can it all be fine

Or just be funny?

We hope for a change

We should instead try

Try intent again

No more hope and cry

I Didn't Ask

I didn't ask for this

One day I just got

Can't even do a...

Immune's lost the plot

I woke with weak limbs...

Now my legs are rot

Lucky me, can take this

There're some who can not

We didn't ask for this

Some husband, some Dad

Half the man I was

No good things, no bad things

I'm blinded, because...

Was set, to be great

Then fell, from great height

Wanted that, without gaits

If I Had

If I had a tail

I'd wag all day long

I'd wag in the bath

I'd wag through life's throng

If I had a brain

Brand new, functional

I could walk again

Dance though this turmoil

From illness' rubble

If I had the time

Run from this bubble

Ballet through, so fine

Laugh or Cry

Heart clearly has wings

Heart dearly loves you

Life's joy, my heart brings

From hardship, wings grew

Bladder is stinging

Balance has fallen

My heart's still singing

Can't you hear its call?

My heart ballets 'round

Though stuck to this chair

Heart sings freedom's sound

Do they hear, do they care?

McCartney

There's only, Richard and Paul left
They ran, with the Beatles
George and John too
Carrying 60 weighty, gold discs

It's surprising, but they flew
Paul flew on, with Wings
One could say, he grew
Then the Frog Chorus, was a solo thing

The world still, misses John
George too, now who'll replace, the gone?
With John & George gone, the world is bereft
Not to mention, Mr McCartney

Who surely had, the gladdest of times
Only to reap, the saddest of times
Rich old poor old, Sir Mr McCartney
Will he be, the only one left?

MS

It's all in the mind?

Then gets on one's nerves

Eats away the sight

There's no magpie there

Lots of minute spies

Sense what you enjoy

Like sex? Well that's gone!

Like having a job?

Your work there is done

Early retirement

Driving, commuting

That's not what it meant

Was earning and learning

Retired, but ambitious

Eating but choking

Write but no focus

Cooking, now sitting

Piles for slow bowel

Words straining our voice

Sit there and waste hours

Where's the healthy choice?

Nature

We can't give up now

We have come so far

We must aim Earth's bough

Must raise human bar

Earth's nearly ruined

In furthering ourselves

Nature came second

As dust on our shelves

Nature can resume

Given half the chance

We're not making room

Wasting Earth's last dance?

Grenfell

June 2017

The Tower burnt down

Shocked! I could have cried

I feel sick, angry

Generations died

And no more hungry

The children can't cry

In that flat down stairs

Old, no more cranky

I sit thinking, 'Why?'

Anger grows in me

Red tape, with reason

But they tore it up

Economies of treason

Lives or more mark-up?

Let death just breeze in.

Near Distance

Pulled into Egypt

Looked at pyramids

Too poor to make one

Robbed a tomb, instead

Sailed to Australia

Blacks are getting drunk

Just like white people

Just as drunk kerplunk

They worshiped nature

They have gained nothing

We are still trying

To reclaim what we stole

All living in peace

Thriving with nature

Then feeling white heat

Ransacked, raped, tortured

Sea King sailed the seas

Distance became near

Sea King's on its knees

Distance coming clear

Nobodies

All of the nobodies

We really need them

Really they are somebody

Are we all nobodies?

Longing for that somebody?

Set in rose gold frieze

There nobodies stay

As flowers on the wall

True love sways, give way

Nuclear

Disaster's still there?

They hold on to bombs

Do they, don't they, care?

One day, could be gone

Takes one finger, bare

Shaky finger, all done

Shaky leader dares

Why, oh why, ?

Collected symbols

Then binned them, right on!

Still lacking courage

To get rid, new-clear gone

Will take real braves in big halls

Planet Earth is green

They haven't even seen

From outer-space it's blue

Hope big-button fingers are true

New powers are keen

Life there is too cheap

Who'd press death's button

Finish all life?

To live is to give.

Pick a Flag

Dave lives in Downing Street
So does Rt. Hon. Clegg
Blair's already fixed us up
The problems can't be them

Easterners, mid-easterners
Just pick a flag, it's them
EU, Foreign Markets
Who can we blame today?

Surely not the largest
PC rules mean less targets
Dave's still in Downing Street
So is Rt. Hon. Clegg

We're all still here ok
Some poor souls are lying dead

Rainbows

Rainbows keep falling at my feet

But I'm not a pot of gold

My good fortune seems complete

To our two sons, I'm old

To me, I've luck like Farouche

Sight failing, I'm old as I feel

And as young as I look

I feel fine and free, like rainbows.

Regret

All regret something

Be it big or small

Maybe a gold ring

Perhaps football scores

Did you give wrong shout?

Or miss true calling?

Throw yourself about?

Was your engine stalling?

What's your real regret?

Just remember this

You wake each morning

You can poo and wee

What will be, will be

Efforts never waste

Life's no sad bad game

Ne'er too late to change.

Remember Free

Do you, I or we

Remember Free?

Relive memories

Late nights, late mornings

Booze fuelled, late nights

Body filled, late mornings

Soul filled, late nights

Do you, I or we

Remember Free?

Sale

Christmas sale OFF OFF OFF

January sale then

Easter's next, save as you eat

Spend obese while you scoff

Christmas pud or mince-meat

Mini-eggs & sweet bunny

Forget God's son & tuck in to the feast

It's not about them but your money

In retail, holidays are aggressive

Cards not cheap, bills not funny

But the sales aren't impressive

Not like Holidays, happy tummy.

Secondary

No more remission

Only going slower

My old condition

Now it's twenty one

Free constipation

Reduced having fun

Frustration, clear win

Now I'm near sighted

But still in the pink?

And a bit frightened.

Seen Me

I have seen me around

The loosening skin

The waistline unfound

Laughing to the brim.

I have seen me around

Slowly growing older

My recall ran aground

While becoming colder.

I have seen me around

I still fit in my skin

Would love to skip, bound

I have seen me around.

Seize The Day

Celebrate, rejoice

We are here to live

Really, we've no choice

But to share joy, give

We have not died yet

Luck wastes no second

Live to reach up high

Brave to be reckoned.

Smiles

Open up your will
Big heart, and smile
It's to share and thrill

Anybody for miles of smiles
At least a feeling of good will
Young or old, long or short while

We all love our smiles
Lucky lives, feel wonderful
Your smile, best for miles.

Sneezes

Sneezes are contagious
Like germs or like yawns.
Snoring is outrageous
To listeners not to snores
Turning sleep's gilded pages.

Smiles are contagious
They can laugh out loud
Smiles aren't outrageous
They spread joy around!
Spread fun amongst us! :-)

Soul

They can fix bodies
Amputate, medicate
One day, make copies
One day, replicate.

They replace sockets
Remove rolls & lumps
That's all so sweet
But one thing's not done

You must hold your soul
Try to stay neat
They can't fix a soul.
Be tidy, no retreat
Make your soul complete.

Stars

When the stars fell down

Off fell monkey's crowns.

The Moon ran around

As the Earth just frowned.

The short-sighted clowns

"Now where can we aim?

Surely can't aim down?"

So clowns aim down for shame

Now at sea, stars light

Dancing, romancing,

Reflecting, all night

Enchanted, stars sing.

Sticks

Sticks are not sticky

Not only, leaves leave

Flicks do not flicker

Father had to leave.

Cancer, died in bed

Cancer, didn't leave

Like kicks to our heads

Unshed tears still grieve.

Stop

Crawling, traffic jam

Dozens of miles long

Road works, months long

Car crash, mobile phone

Conversation, obsession.

Dying forests, city smog

There was an outcry, then it stopped.

Shifting sands, Gulf Stream's gone

Just conversing, on and on

P.M.Qs, as children, mock.

Teenage Kicks

Had my ten seconds

Up there in limelight

Sooner than reckoned

Now here, in hindsight.

I wish I'd enjoyed,

Enjoyed what I had.

Young, fit, and sampled

More of what life has.

Tasted finer things

Chased that extra mile

Loved more, ring-a-ding,

Before I knew the piles.

The Beginning

If it was, 'big bang'...

Before that moment

Then never again

There was symmetry

Order fell to harangue

Not wars but massacres

Look what came to banks

A, B, C, Two, One, Three

What has come to be?

Order to anarchy?

The Coin, Tossed

We have tossed our coin

Our cards have been dealt

Emotions went boyng

Repercussions, felt

All bets were taken

Our strides have been strode

World's still unshaken

Time to crack the code?

We have tossed our coin

What now but to deal?

Never been before?

How d'you think we feel?

The Fortune

We are all born rich

We start with fortunes

Our own birthright

We were important.

There for the wasting

All time in the world

Just human nature

Burning, flags unfurled.

Then mean time reclaims

We'd too much, too soon

Race unwaxed, race wanes

Humans race, to lose?

The Game of Life

We've won the game

Won a lifetime

With free air and sun

Plus the lifelong grime.

First childish boredom

Then aged apathy

The office 'whoredom'
Life's 'Regret to be.'

But always, blue sky
Feeling the free sun
We're free to learn why
The game of life is won.

The God Within

We all love our self

Start to end, the best

The mind, the brain's wealth

Some forget the rest,

Even mental health.

God's within us all

Need an outside church?

They built temples tall!

Praying 'till it hurt

Just for when we fall.

Nobody answers

No-one's bloody there

Just internal voice

All can, and should, care.

Religions, fantasy?

Just very well told

One's will, has to be

Never pale, but bold.

The Other Side

Their grass is greener

On the other side

Their air is cleaner

Can we hitch that ride?

Their sky is bluer

On the other side

Their truth is truer

If we climb this slide.

The clouds are empty

There's no threat of rain

On the other side

Their lives are good again.

The Sun

The Sun is always shining
We're just waiting
For cloud to stop baiting
Hear tiny insects, whining

Over all, infants crying
Live volcanoes, roaring
On homeless, ill pining
Ocean waves, crash, soaring

Sun lit breeze gently snores
Hospitals, sighing
Grass, daisies growing
Our Sun knows it best
There hot, mutely lonely.

This MS

I have that MS

This MS, has me.

My optic nerve's gone

But why can't *they* see?

Swallowing's no fun

Speech is not easy

It is not too late

Will this let me be?

Lonely, we're lonely

Oh why, must *it* be?

Depressed, but I laugh

Flashes, of despair

What is the punch line?

Can't find it anywhere.

Will a cure appear?

In my dream, it's here!

This New England

When can you be

You England, for us?

Free, equality

No more Eton mess.

Attractive towns and cities

No more pomp pretence.

No lonely towns

No more bridges burnt

Some have plastic crowns

Fortunes blown on that tat.

Honest peace will thrive

When will you be live?

Time and Money

Oh! Which one is worse?

Or which one is better?

Easy, without pain?

Hard and without gain?

Winning without shame

Paying, 'Keep the change.'

Which one is your lot?

Everything's in time.

Are money and time

Much good for the soul?

Slowly laugh at all,

That's how money rolls

Whilst time never stops

Rolls on, never off.

Where has it all gone?

Behind, remember?

Shhh few people know...

It's with your money.

Whales Dream Too

In fact, we all do.

All mammals have dreams,,

Dogs, cats, kangaroo.

We think sleep and dream

Tonight, so will you.

As whales float and dream

Perhaps dream, of you

As you dream, you two.

Young At Heart

If you're young at heart

You're forever young.

But nearly forty

I worry it'll be too hard

To stay young at heart.

I know time, like an old friend.

When this poem is finished

I'll be older than its start

But not more worried

I am 'Young at heart'

I am time's old friend.

Séan

Séan, we want to thank you

For shining your light on here.

You're lucky, and us too,

A lifetime since you got here.

Oh smiling, tranquil you

Never known it wrong

Find or lose religion

Will drink the wine, sing the songs

With out love, without condition,

You'll never know it wrong

Beautiful and innocent

While you grow big and strong

Live life of magnificence

About Séan Phillip Tanner – the day that your first piece of post arrived

About The Author

I was diagnosed with Multiple Sclerosis at 23. In the year 2000. The millennium could only get better and in my own style it did.

I married my beautiful Helen in 2005 and Séan was born in 2013 then Daniel in 2015. Our wonderful sons make our lives and our family complete.

Poetry is a great outlet for my thoughts and emotions. I hope that this book may one day help my sons to cope with life's slings and arrows and understand my life with MS.

Printed in Great Britain
by Amazon

56814483R00059